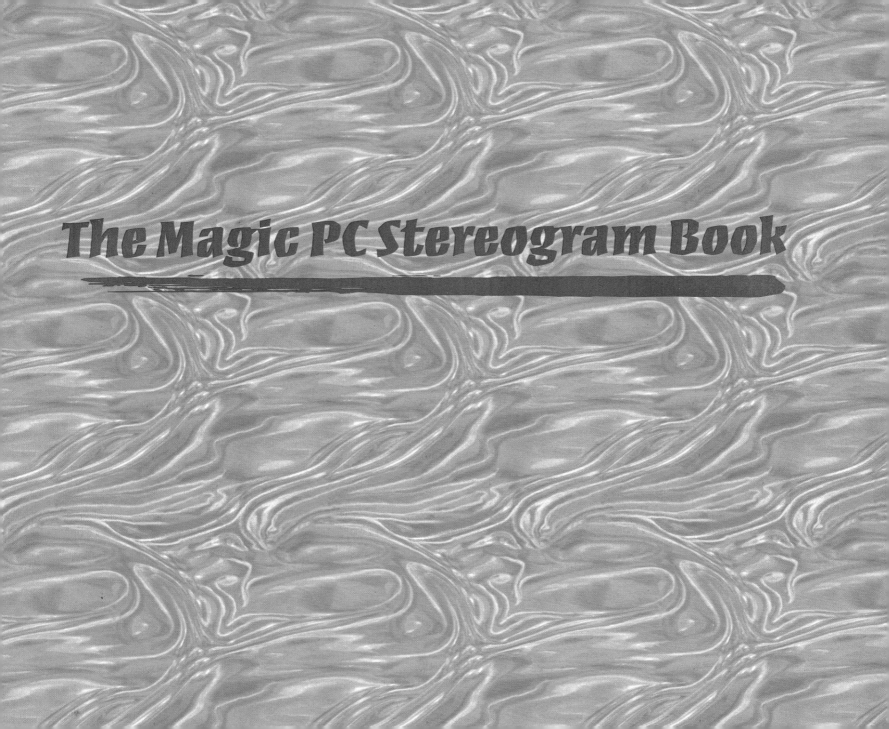

The Magic PC Stereogram Book

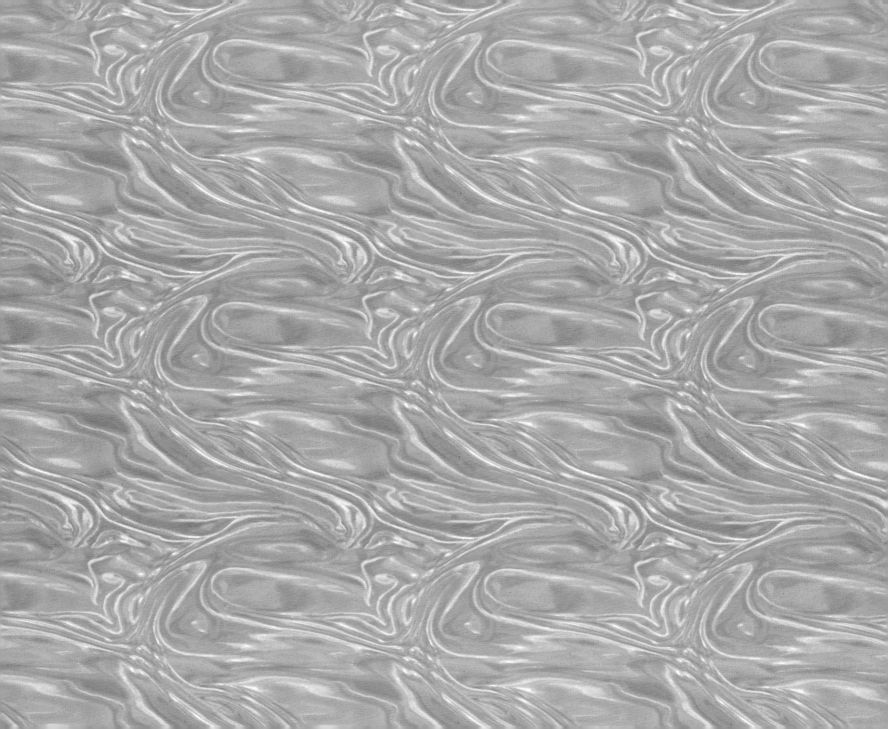

The Magic PC Stereogram Book

DANIEL SILLESCU

Translated by Sabine Fabian and Guy Hart-Davis

SYBEX

San Francisco · Paris · Düsseldorf · Soest

Acquisitions Editor: Kristine Plachy
Developmental Editor: Stefan B. Lipson
Editor: Peter Weverka
Technical Editor: Daniel A. Tauber
Book Design & Page Layout:
    Penn&Ink ♦ George Mattingly Design
Production Assistant: Janet K. Boone
Cover Designer: Joanna Kim Gladden

Screen reproductions produced with Collage Plus.
Collage Plus is a trademark of Inner Media Inc.

SYBEX is a registered trademark of SYBEX Inc.

This book was first published under the title *Versteckte Bilder selbstgemacht am PC* copyright © 1994 SYBEX Verlag GmbH, Düsseldorf, Germany.

Library of Congress Card Number: 94-69733

ISBN: 0-7821-1662-0

MANUFACTURED IN THE UNITED STATES OF AMERICA

10 9 8 7 6 5 4 3 2 1

The Magic PC Stereogram Book

CONTENTS OF THE BOOK

This book presents examples of stereograms and instructions for producing them.
You'll learn how to make:

WHAT'S ON THE COMPANION DISK

The companion disk contains RDSdraw 2.1, a program for creating your own 3-D images on the PC and hiding them in stereograms. With RDSdraw, you can create and view your own stereograms on screen!

Preface

Stereograms are all the rage these days. If you've seen these 3-D effects and you want to try your hand at making them, buy this book and get right down to it.

In this book, I'll show you the different kinds of stereograms you can make. I'll tell you how each kind works and I'll describe how you can develop your own images on the PC. Right now, you don't need special software to make 3-D images. For example, you can produce text stereograms with any text editor or word-processing program. You can even use the EDIT program that comes with DOS.

This book includes a disk with the public-domain program RDSdraw. Using this program, you can produce your own 3-D images on the PC and hide them automatically behind a random-dot pattern or an artistic pattern in just a few seconds.

What's most exciting of all is being able to produce 3-D effects on your own screen. Many people find on-screen stereograms easier to see than stereograms in books.

No doubt you'll want to print out your own magic images (either in color or in black and white). Then you'll have truly original works with which to amaze your friends.

Daniel Sillescu
Mainz, August 1994

Installing RDSdraw

First, you need to install the RDSdraw files on the companion disk on your hard drive. Then you'll be ready to look at the examples in this book and produce your own stereograms. You'll be able to produce 3-D images by using the drawing program and hide those images inside a pattern.

Here's how to install RDSdraw on your hard disk:

❶ Insert the floppy disk in the appropriate drive on your computer.

❷ Go to the floppy disk drive (A or B) by entering one of these commands:

    A:↵

    B:↵

❸ Install the program by entering one of these commands:

    INSTALLA↵

    INSTALLB↵

Wait while the installation program copies the files onto your hard disk and decompresses them. When it is finished, you'll be on the C drive and in a new directory that RDSdraw created. The directory is called MAGIC. You should see this prompt on your screen:

    C:\MAGIC>

❹ Make sure the files have been installed successfully on your hard disk by typing the following:

    DIR↵

You should see a list of these files on your screen:

README	TXT
RDSDRAW	EXE
HELLO	TXT
WAVES	TGA
GEOMETRY	TGA
VOLCANO	TGA
STAR	TGA

Starting RDSdraw

L et's look at how to start RDSdraw. If you just installed the program, you should still be in the correct subdirectory (C:\MAGIC\), so you can simply enter the following command to start RDSdraw:

RDSDRAW⏎

If you're not in the C:\MAGIC\ subdirectory (for example, if you're working in a different directory or you are on a different drive), enter the following three lines to start RDSdraw:

C:⏎
CD\MAGIC⏎
RDSDRAW⏎

tip You need use the first of these commands, C:⏎, only if you're working on a different drive than C. If you're already on C, you don't need to enter it (but it won't hurt if you do).

Exiting RDSdraw

The rest of this book discusses how to use RDSdraw. Meanwhile, you need to know how to exit the program. It's really simple: Just press the Esc key. RDSdraw will prompt you as follows:

Do you really want to leave?

Type Y (for Yes) to exit RDSdraw. (If you pressed Esc by mistake, type N to return to RDSdraw.)

Text Stereograms in Seconds

To see why stereograms look three-dimensional, let's try a little experiment with Figure 1. Hold the picture in front of your eyes and try viewing it using either the cross-eyed technique or the parallel technique.

➡ The cross-eyed technique: Cross your eyes (if you can) and look at the picture, but don't concentrate on any particular part.

➡ The parallel technique: Try to look right through the book, making sure your eyes are looking straight ahead independently of one another.

Whichever technique you use, the picture should go blurry within a moment or two. Very slowly move the book away from your

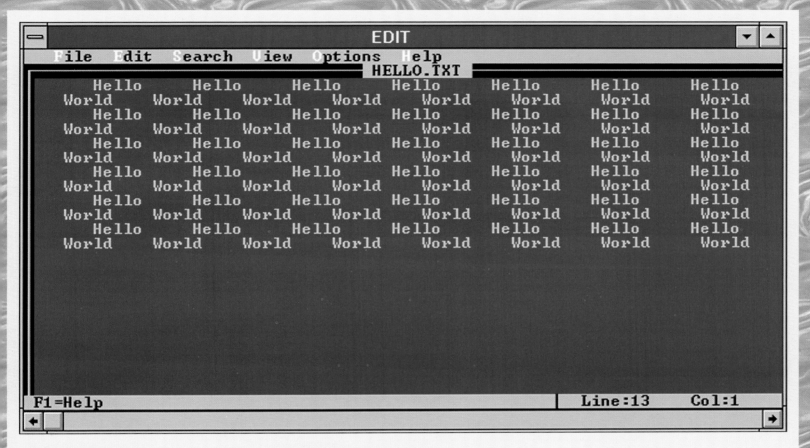

Figure 1: Hello World, a text stereogram with two spatial layers

face (at about half an inch every second). Do you see the 3-D effect?

The "Hellos" move backward three-dimensionally, while the "Worlds" seem to shift more into the foreground.

Did you ever think you could see a three-dimensional image so easily?

How It Works

No one can deny the effect of repetition. Just think of chanting, in which one word is spoken again and again to induce a certain state. More to our purpose, the repetition of images—with slight variations among those images—can create the illusion of three dimensions. Sir David Brewster (he invented the kaleidoscope) discovered this in 1844 while experimenting with pattern elements. Brewster found that varying the size of the elements, varying their shape, and varying the distance between them created a 3-D effect.

The eye automatically projects two words arranged parallel with each other into a three-dimensional plane. Because each "Hello" in our example figure was separated by five spaces and each "World" was separated by only four, we saw two different three-dimensional levels.

The line below presents—as far as I know—the simplest stereogram around. Take a look at this line using the parallel technique or the cross-eyed technique. You will see the same effect you saw in Figure 1.

Hello   Hello Hello   Hello

How to Do It

I'll bet you're ready to produce your own text stereogram, one with your first and last name, perhaps. Few things could be simpler:

❶ Switch on your PC and load the DOS text editor named EDIT.COM (it is included with DOS Versions 5.0 and higher). To load the DOS text editor, enter

EDIT↵

Alternatively, you can load any text-editing or word-processing program, such as Microsoft Word or WordPerfect.

❷ Press ↵ five times, then type five spaces and your first name.

❸ Press the spacebar ten times, then type your first name again. Keep doing this until the line is almost full.

④ Press ↵ to move to the next line, then type your last name and press the spacebar nine times.

⑤ Repeat step 4 until the line is full, and press ↵ to finish the line. Click with the mouse and drag to select both lines of text, then choose Edit ❯ Copy.

⑥ Click to place the cursor on the next empty line, then choose Edit ❯ Paste. Keep choosing Edit ❯ Paste until the screen is almost completely full of text. Your screen should now look something like this:

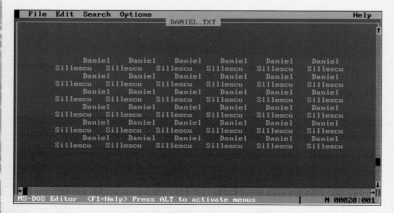

If you stare at your screen using either the cross-eyed technique or the parallel technique, you should experience the same three-dimensional effect that you saw with the "Hello World" example in Figure 1.

tip If you don't see the 3-D effect in Figure 1, try loading the ASCII file HELLO TXT (which you'll find in the directory C:\MAGIC\) into the DOS text editor or into your text-editing or word-processing program. It's much easier to see magic images on the screen than on paper.

Making Text Stereograms with WYSIWYG Applications

As we've seen, placing two different amounts of space between words produces two three-dimensional levels. Likewise, you can produce several three-dimensional levels by working with different spacing in a text stereogram.

Take a look at Figure 2. You should be able to see four different layers, as described below.

➡ The yellow "Nevers" seems to have receded into the background. The space between each word is 5 cm.

➡ The "SAYs" in the second line have only 4.5 cm. between them. That's why the second line seems to be further forward three-dimensionally than the line with the yellow "Nevers."

➡ The orange "Nevers," which are only 4 cm. apart, appear even further forward in the picture.

➡ With their 3.5-cm. spacing, the red "agains" are clearly in the foreground, while the following repetitions with wider spacing slowly recede into the background.

While you can produce a multilevel stereogram by using the DOS text editor, you'll find that you can get more even impressive results by working with word-processing applications that offer different on-screen fonts and colors. The next section discusses how Figure 2 was put together.

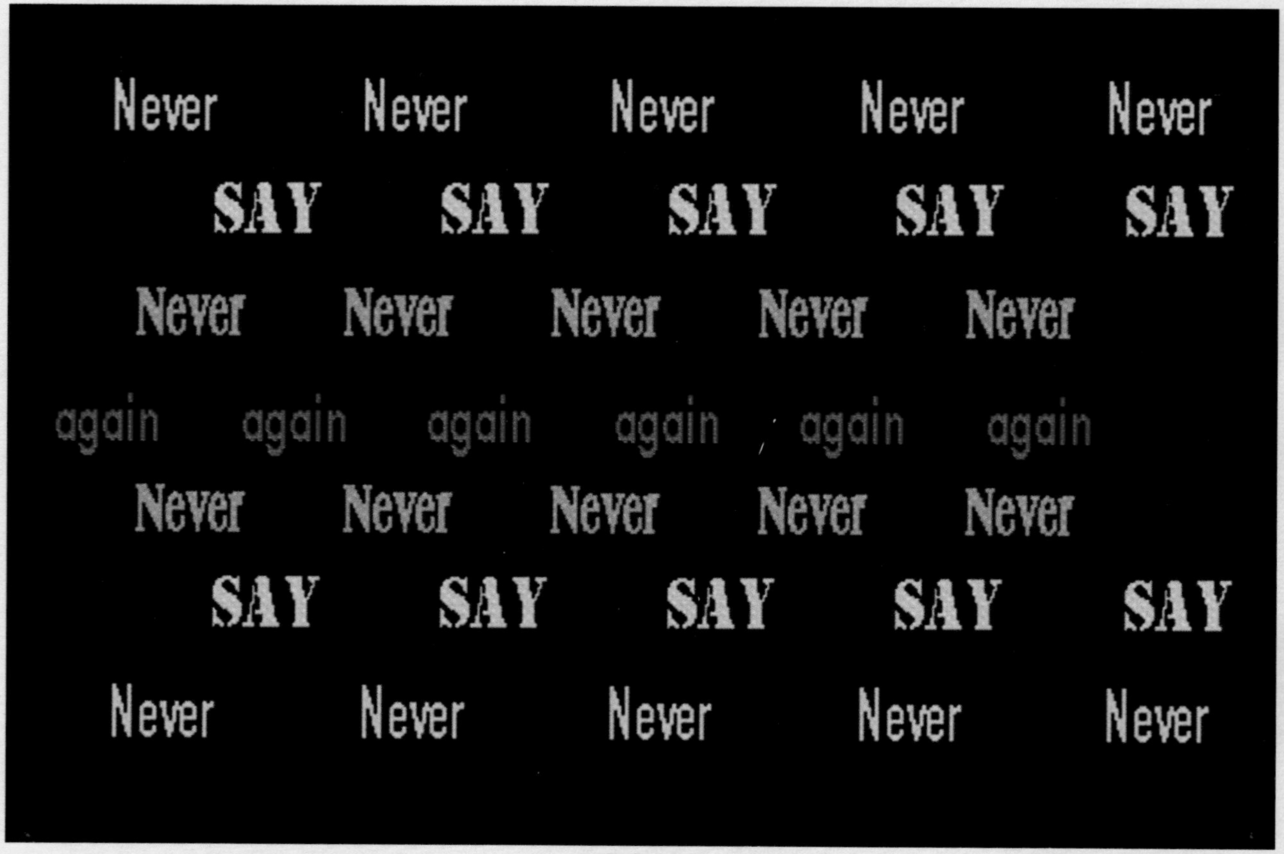

Figure 2: Never Say Never Again, a WYSIWYG text stereogram with four spatial layers

How to Do It

Here's how I put together Figure 2:

❶ I used Adobe Photoshop to create a black background.

❷ I typed in the words *Never, SAY, Never,* and *again* in different fonts and colors one under the other. I offset these words and changed their widths to make it easier to calculate the spaces between them (as seen at the top of the next column).

❸ I selected the topmost word and then duplicated it by using the Ctrl-C and Ctrl-V commands. I then dragged the copy exactly 5 cm. to the right. I repeated the procedure with the other three words (see top left, next page).

❹ I then duplicated and copied the words on the other lines in the same way, except that I moved them by 4.5, 4, and 3.5 cm., respectively.

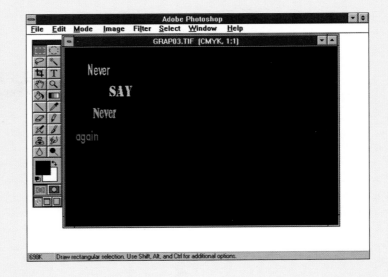

❺ To avoid having to repeat step 4 for the three lines at the bottom, I used the Ctrl-C command to copy the three lines as a whole.

❻ I then was able to copy all three lines to the lower part of the screen (see top right, next page).

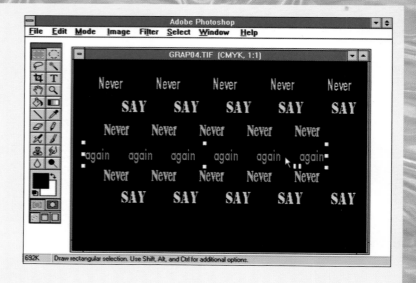

tip If you don't have Adobe Photo-shop, you can still produce similar text stereo-grams with other graphics programs, such as CorelDRAW!. You can even use WYSIWYG word-processing programs, such as Word for Windows.

The Joy of Repetition: Stereogram Wallpaper

A three-dimensional effect in a stereogram produced by pattern elements repeated continuously is called stereogram wallpaper. You could also apply this term to the two text stereograms in Figures 1 and 2, although normally stereogram wallpaper consists of images rather than text.

Take a look at Figure 3 using either the cross-eyed technique or the parallel technique. After a while, you'll notice that one row of cherries recedes into the background, while the next row comes more to the foreground, and so on.

The principle is the same as with text stereograms, except that this time we are dealing with graphical elements rather than text:

➡ In the first row, the space between the cherries is 4 cm.

➡ In the second row, you see exactly the same cherries, but this time they are only 3.5 cm. apart.

Figure 3: "Cherry-ogram" wallpaper, with two spatial layers

How to Do It

The picture with the cherries was created in CorelDRAW. But I also used a program called Painter from Fractal Design, because the program is so much fun. Here are the steps I took to create Figure 3.

❶ I used Painter to create a bright-red cherry and saved in PCX format.

❷ I drew a rectangle in CorelDRAW and filled it with yellow and white.

❸ I used the File ❯ Import command to import the PCX graphic of the cherry into the picture, and I shrank the cherry a little.

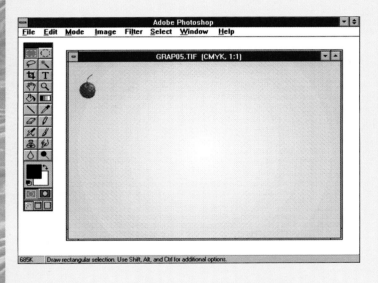

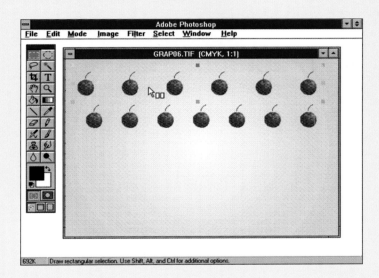

④ I duplicated the cherry using the Ctrl-C and Ctrl-V commands. Then I moved each copy of it 4 cm. to the right.

⑤ I moved another copy of the cherry to an offset position under the first row, then made further copies, which I moved only 3.5 cm. to the right.

⑥ I marked one row of cherries, grouped them, copied the group, and then moved the copies lower down the screen.

Where Are You Sitting in the First Row?

Of course, you can also produce stereogram wallpaper with more than two 3-D levels. For example, look at Figure 4 and try to figure out which of the armchairs or chairs in the first row

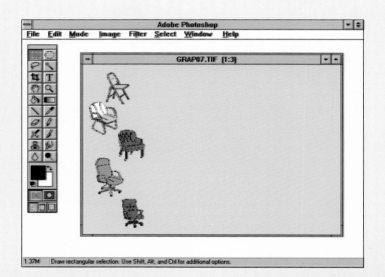

Figure 4: Where are you sitting in the first row? (A stereogram wallpaper with five spatial layers.)

you're sitting in. The graphic on page 22 shows the four original chairs.

tip Once you've studied the examples given so far in this book, you shouldn't need step-by-step descriptions to make them any longer. If you're searching for possible images to use in your stereograms, remember that the clip-art libraries of most graphics programs provide a rich source of graphics.

Random-Dot Stereograms in Black and White

That's enough of simple text stereograms and stereogram wallpaper. The next four images we'll look at and create were produced by using RDSdraw, the public-domain program on the companion disk included with this book. The four images have two things in common:

➡ They are real random-dot stereograms. The image, which emerges as a three-dimensional image when you look at the picture the right way, is not visible at first—it's hidden by an automatically generated random-dot pattern.

➡ All four images were produced as black-and-white stereograms. They are less attractive than color stereograms, but because they're black and white, at least you can print them if you don't have a color printer.

How to Do It

To produce random-dot stereograms, start RDSdraw and draw the hidden image the same way you would using an ordinary drawing program. Try the following example:

❶ First click on the Text tool, then click in the middle of the left side of the black drawing area.

❷ Type your first name and press ↵. Your name will appear in white. (See the illustration on page 26.)

❸ Click on the OK button. Answer the prompt by typing N and pressing ↵, then confirm the choice Black/White RDS by pressing ↵ again. RDSdraw will start producing the dot pattern.

❹ As soon as the computer has generated the dot pattern, try searching for your first name on the screen, using either the cross-eyed technique or the parallel technique. You should see your first name

RDSdraw - (C) 1994 Johannes Schmid   [ROUND]

tip After you exit RDSdraw, you'll find the file you just created under the name NONAME.TGA in the \MAGIC directory. You can print this file by using a graphics program such as the shareware program PaintShop Pro for Windows or a commercial graphics program like CorelDRAW!.

appearing in the foreground because every color represents a layer in the three-dimensional view.

❺ If you want to save the stereogram in a file so that you can print it later on, press any key, type Y, and press ↵ to accept the suggested file name, NONAME.

The Sample Pictures

I'm sure you'd like to know what you can see in the four sample pictures and how these pictures were produced. Here's a brief description of how I made Figures 5, 6, 7, and 8.

➡ For Figure 5, I used the Load button to load the file named WAVES.

➡ Figure 6 shows a wave motif too, but this time I used the palette in PaintShop Pro to change the color in the black-and-white stereogram. Opposite is a shot of the palette.

➡ The word White is hidden inside Figure 7. To brighten up the random-dot pattern, I started RDSdraw with the this command, which makes 20 percent of the dots in the pattern black:

RDSDRAW /RDSPERC=20.⏎

➡ For Figure 8, I loaded RDSdraw using a similar command to the one above, except this time I

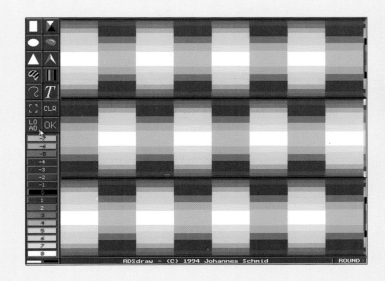

used the value 80 to make the dot pattern 80 percent black:

RDSDRAW /RDSPERC=80.⏎

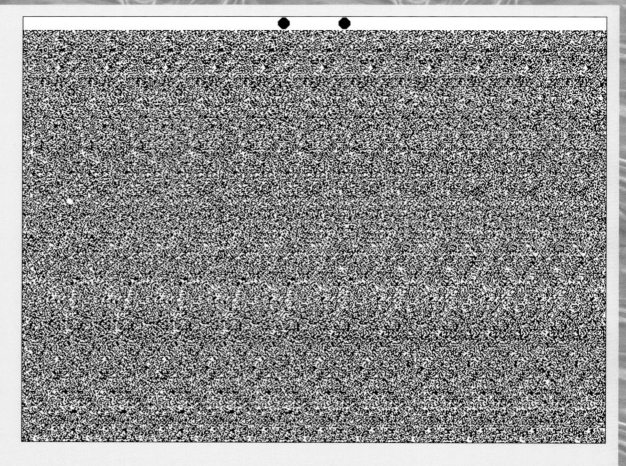

Figure 5: Waves, a black-and-white stereogram with sixteen spatial layers

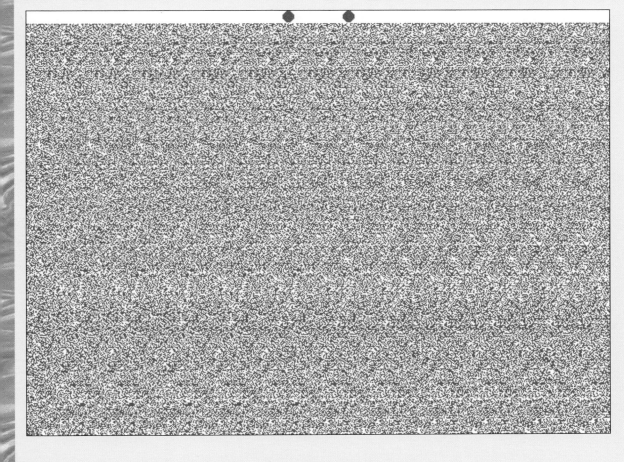

Figure 6: Waves, a color-shifted black-and-white stereogram

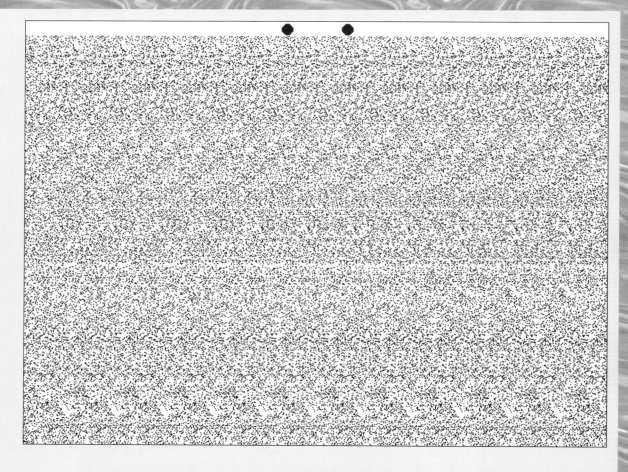

Figure 7: White, a black-and-white stereogram with only 20 percent black

Figure 8: Black, a black-and-white stereogram with 80 percent black

Multicolored Random-Dot Stereograms

Do you have access to a color printer? Do you at least want to view your own random-dot stereograms in color onscreen? After clicking the OK button in RDSdraw to generate your stereogram, all you have to do is make another choice from a menu.

Let's look at how to create 4-color and 16-color stereograms.

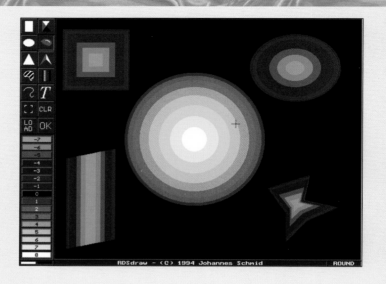

FOUR-COLOR STEREOGRAMS

The image above is hidden behind the four-color random-dot stereogram shown in Figure 9 on page 34. To achieve this effect with RDSdraw, follow these steps:

❶ Click on the Load button and delete the word NONAME by pressing Backspace six times.

❷ Type the file name GEOMETRY in place of NONAME and press ↵.

❸ Click on the OK button, answer the prompt by typing N, and choose 4-Color RDS from the menu by typing V.

❹ Now all you have to do is press ↵ twice, and the 4-color random-dot stereogram that you see in Figure 9 will appear on your screen.

tip To save the picture, press any key and answer the question by typing Y. Delete the suggested name GEOMETRY by pressing Backspace, enter a name of your choice (for example, test1), and press ↵. After you exit RDSdraw, you'll find the graphics file TEST1.TGA (or whatever name you gave it) in the directory \MAGIC. You can then print the file by using a graphics program such as PaintShop Pro.

Figure 9: Geometry, a four-color random-dot stereogram

16-Color Stereograms

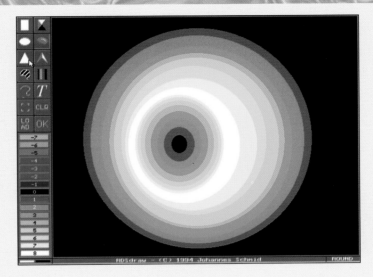

The volcano illustrated to the right is hidden behind the 16-color random-dot stereogram in Figure 10 on page 36. You can easily produce this image on your own, because the version of RDSdraw that comes on the companion disk includes the sample graphic VOLCANO.TGA from which the volcano was made.

To create a random-dot stereogram similar to the one in Figure 10:

❶ Click on the Load button again and delete the suggested file name by pressing the Backspace key.

❷ Enter VOLCANO instead and press ↵ twice.

❸ Click on the OK button, answer the prompt by typing N, and choose 16-Color RDS from the menu by typing V.

❹ Press ↵ twice, and the random-dot stereogram will be generated.

As in the previous example, you can save it under another file name if you want to print it later on.

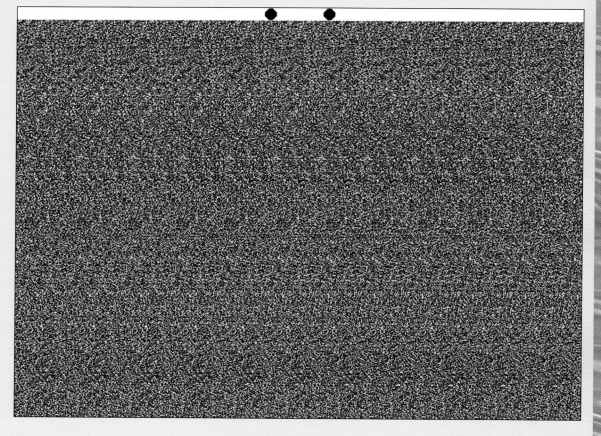

Figure 10: Volcano, a 16-color random-dot stereogram

Creating Your Own Images

Needless to say, you needn't depend on sample graphics to produce color stereograms. By using the drawing tools in RDSdraw, you can develop your own images and then hide them. For example, try clicking the 3-D Sphere button and dragging the mouse to draw a circle. You'll be surprised at the result....

tip For a complete description of the full range of tools that RDSdraw provides, turn to the *RDSdraw Reference* section at the back of this book.

Artistic Patterns in Full Color

All the pictures I've shown you so far were text stereograms (Figures 1 and 2), stereogram wallpaper (Figures 3 and 4), or random-dot stereograms (Figures 5 through 10). All these stereograms, especially the random-dot ones, impress the viewer with their hidden three-dimensional images, but they look pretty boring when viewed as two-dimensional images.

You've probably seen stereograms that have a real artistic value even when seen in only two dimensions. The reason these stereograms look so good is because beautiful patterns were used in the foreground.

You can achieve these effects with RDSdraw. The program lets you hide 3-D images behind an artistic pattern—even a full-color pattern. (However, your computer hardware must be able to support these kinds of graphics.)

Sample Images

I've prepared two examples of artistic patterns in full color. You can display these images on your screen if you want to.

➡ The star that you can see in the illustration below is hidden behind Figure 11 (page 40). To generate this image with RDSdraw, load the STAR

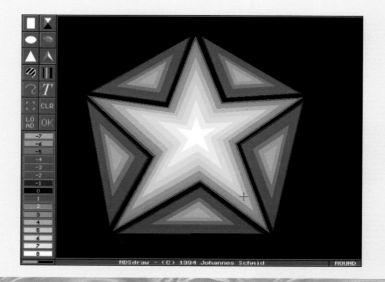

model file, click on the OK button, and choose Super Color RDS from the menu.

➡ I'm sorry to say you can't directly reproduce the skeleton shown below. It was produced with another drawing program and then imported into RDSdraw. It is hidden inside Figure 12 (page 41).

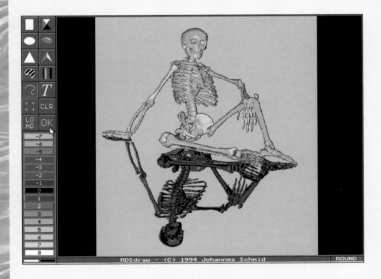

tip You can change the model colors used in a picture. When you choose Super Color RDS from the menu, RDSdraw generates a very pretty pattern—but, unfortunately, always the same pattern. To change patterns for Figure 12, I saved the image and worked on it in PaintShop Pro, using the Colors ❯ Negative Image command. By the way, you can also produce interesting color effects by using the Red/Green/Blue option in the Colors menu.

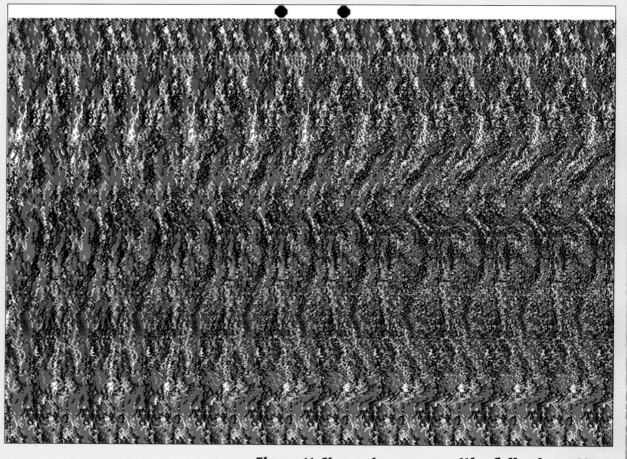

Figure 11: Star, a stereogram with a full-color pattern

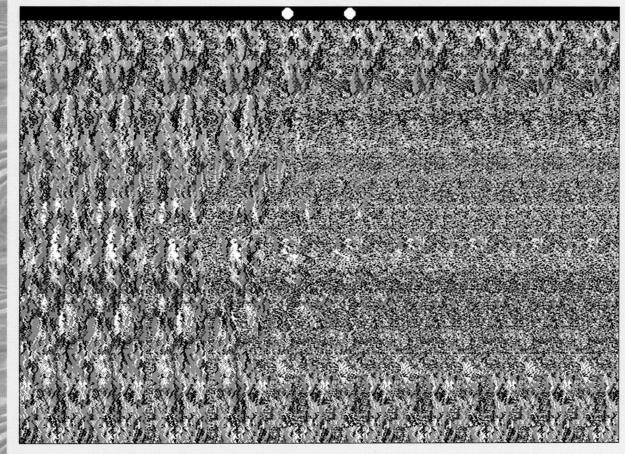

Figure 12: Skeleton, a stereogram with a full-color pattern and color-shifting

How It Works

When you were creating stereogram wallpaper earlier in this book, you produced the three-dimensional effect by varying the spacing between the individual words or pattern elements in the image. But random-dot stereograms do not show any three-dimensional motif when you look at them in two dimensions. At first, it's hard to believe that random-dot stereograms work in the same way as stereogram wallpaper. To show that they do work in the same way, look at the following lines. Every dot in these lines corresponds with a randomly chosen letter:

```
AGMXTRHAGMXTNHAGMXTNHAGMXTNH
AGMXTRHAGMXTNHAGMXTNHAGMXTNH
AGMXTRHAGMXTNHAGMXTNHAGMXTNH
```

The succession AGMXTRH is repeated four times in every line. Now, let's put a letter Q roughly in the middle of the second line so that the letter H at the end of the second line falls out of the frame:

```
AGMXTRHAGMXTNHAGMXTNHAGMXTNH
AGMXTRHAGMXTNHAGQMXTNHAGMXTN
AGMXTRHAGMXTNHAGMXTNHAGMXTNH
```

Exactly at the point where Q is added, the pattern recedes to the background by one layer. The effect disappears in the third line because the letter Q is not repeated.

In the lines below, nothing was added. Instead, the letter M was deleted in the second line, and the letter A was inserted again in the remaining space on the right side of the line. The result? The second line comes more to the foreground, turning the effect around. Now, imagine having dots instead of letters, and you'll understand how random-dot stereograms work.

```
AGMXTRHAGMXTNHAGMXTNHAGMXTNH
AGMXTRHAGMXTNHAGXTNHAGMXTNHA
AGMXTRHAGMXTNHAGMXTNHAGMXTNH
```

Complex Stereograms: The Picture-in-Picture Method

It's a pity that RDSdraw places only one pattern at your disposal. Fortunately, there's a shareware program named Stareogram Generator that produces individual images in two dimensions and that shows them as a completely different image in three dimensions.

tip The Stareogram Generator program is not included on the companion disk for two reasons—it requires additional software and it is tricky to use. Look for it online if you're interested.

Using the Stareogram Generator Program

R ead the following step-by-step instructions to learn how to produce the images hidden behind the stereograms shown in Figures 13 and 14. These images were made with the Stareogram Generator program.

Stareogram Generator is controlled by an INI file (STAREOGM.INI) that you can edit with the DOS editor. Above right is an example of a Stareogram Generator INI file.

❶ The first thing you have to do is indicate in the INI file which TGA graphics file is to be hidden in the magic image. For Figures 13 and 14, I decided to use the head shown opposite.

❷ Stareogram Generator also needs to know which TGA file to use as the wallpaper pattern.

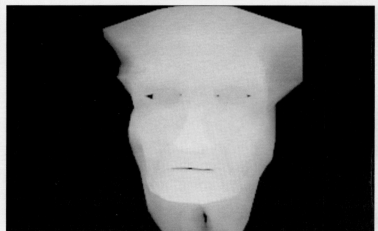

This pattern can be any image strip, as shown here. The wallpaper patterns in Figures 13 and 14 (pages 46 and 47) were produced using Fractal Design Painter, because this program offers pattern functions for repeating images.

❸ Finally, you need to enter the name for the stereogram you're producing. Then you can save the INI file and load the program.

After a mere ten seconds or so, Stareogram Generator will produce a TGA graphic that you can view and print in a graphics program like Paint-Shop Pro.

RDSdraw Reference

Finally, let's take a look at the program on the companion disk, RDSdraw. If you've used other drawing programs—shareware programs like NeoPaint, or freebies like Windows Paintbrush, or high-level graphics packages like Adobe Photoshop, CorelDRAW!, or Fractal Design Painter—you should have no trouble whatsoever handling RDSdraw. But if you need to find out how the specific elements of the program work, I've provided a complete listing of the RDSdraw tools on the following pages.

tip If you're not sure what I mean when I say 3-D pyramid, take a look at Figure 15 (page 48), which includes a labeled screen showing all the elements of RDSdraw.

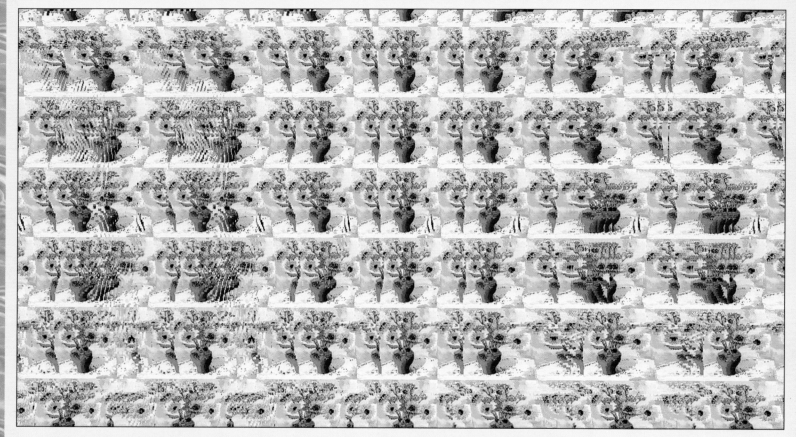

Figure 13: Behind the Flowers, a stereogram produced using the Stareogram Generator and Fractal Design Painter programs

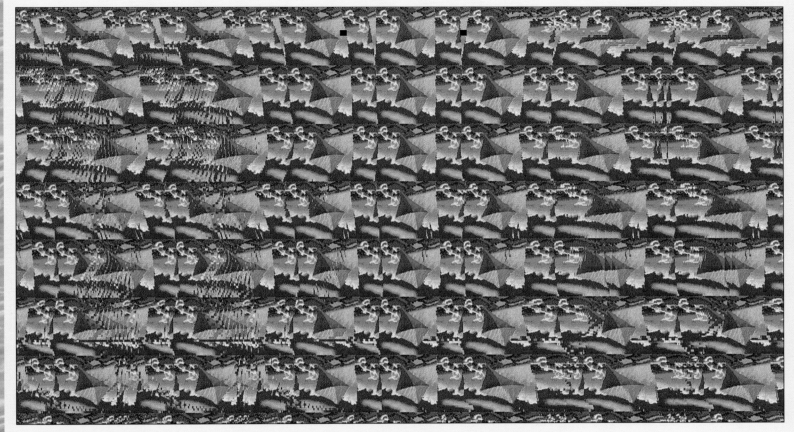

Figure 14: Behind the Kites, a stereogram produced using the Stareogram Generator and Fractal Design Painter programs

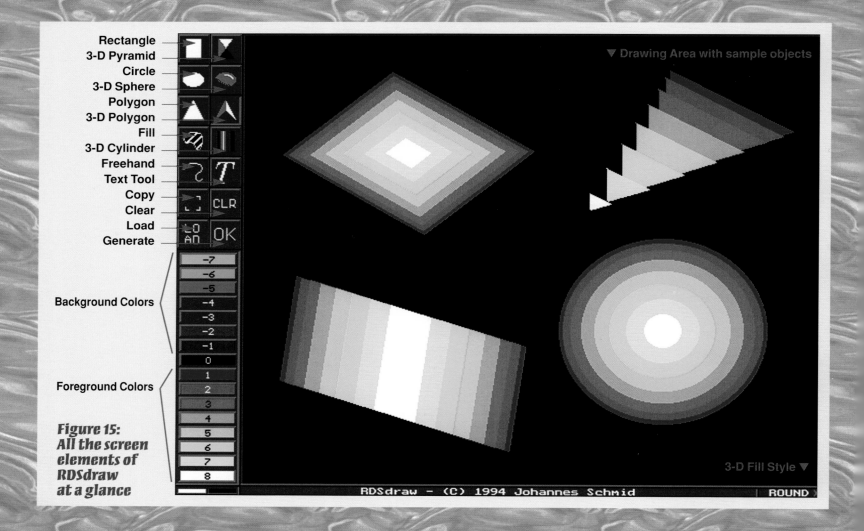

Rectangle
3-D Pyramid
Circle
3-D Sphere
Polygon
3-D Polygon
Fill
3-D Cylinder
Freehand
Text Tool
Copy
Clear
Load
Generate

CLR

LO
AD

OK

Background Colors

-7
-6
-5
-4
-3
-2
-1
0

Foreground Colors

1
2
3
4
5
6
7
8

Figure 15: All the screen elements of RDSdraw at a glance

▼ Drawing Area with sample objects

3-D Fill Style ▼

RDSdraw - (C) 1994 Johannes Schmid

ROUND

RECTANGLE

To draw a rectangle or a parallelogram filled with the currently selected color, click on the Rectangle tool, then click the left mouse button on the page to start drawing. Next, release the mouse button, move the mouse to draw the rectangle in the shape you want, and click to fix the rectangle in place.

3-D PYRAMID

You draw a 3-D pyramid in the same way you draw a rectangle or parallelogram. RDSdraw doesn't fill the 3-D pyramid with the current color, but rather with a multi-layered gradient fill that will create the pyramid effect in the stereogram later.

CIRCLE

To draw circles or ellipses filled with the currently selected color, simply click on the circle button, then click in the drawing area.

3-D SPHERE

Drawing a 3-D sphere works in the same way as drawing an ordinary circle, except that when you select the 3-D Sphere tool, RDSdraw fills the circle with a multicolored gradient fill that creates the 3-D effect in the stereogram.

POLYGON

The Polygon tool lets you easily create line objects such as triangles, hexagons, and arrows. Here's how to use the Polygon tool:

❶ Click on the starting point for the polygon.

❷ Draw a straight line to the final point with your mouse.

③ Click on each remaining corner point.

④ Press any key on your keyboard.

RDSdraw then joins the starting point with the last corner point and fills the polygon with the currently selected color.

3-D POLYGONS

To create a polygon consisting of several three-dimensional levels, click on the 3-D Polygon button and proceed as described in the section above. The only difference is that once you've pressed any key to finish the drawing, you need to determine the three-dimensional direction. To finish the object and fill it with the multicolored gradient fill, click quickly with the left mouse button.

FILL

To fill the whole drawing space with a color, click on the color you want, then click on the Fill button. Finally, click anywhere in the drawing space.

WARNING Bear in mind when using the Fill tool that it will fill the *entire* drawing space with the chosen color, rather than an individual object. *Any objects in the drawing space will be lost.*

3-D CYLINDER

To draw a cylinder-shaped, three-dimensional object, click on the 3-D Cylinder button, then follow the instructions for drawing rectangles or parallelograms.

FREEHAND

After clicking on the Freehand button, you can draw objects of any shape by holding down the left mouse button. You can draw curves as well as lines, so you can draw objects like question marks, hearts, and so on.

tip If you click on the freehand symbol with the right mouse button, you can set the thickness of the drawing pencil: Type a value between 1 and 50 and press ↵. To set rectangular line ends instead of rounded line ends, type Y.

TEXT TOOL

To hide any text in a stereogram, click on the Text tool, then click where you want the upper-left corner of the text object to appear. Next, type the text you want. What you type will appear along the bottom of the screen. Press ↵ to enter the text in the drawing area.

tip Click on the Text tool with the right mouse button to choose from ten different font sizes by pressing → or ←. Press ↵ to set the font size, then choose from the 11 fonts (e.g., Gothic, Script), again by pressing → or ←. Again, press ↵ to set your choice. You can then change the thickness of the individual letters by pressing Enter. Again, use → or ← to make changes, and press ↵ to accept the current choice.

COPYING

The Copy button lets you perform four different actions with the mouse:

➡ Copying objects. Click on the Copy button with your left mouse button to copy the currently selected object. You can then click anywhere in the drawing space to copy the object there.

➡ Deleting parts of objects. If, after you copy an object, you click in the drawing space with the right mouse button, you'll get an effect that's hard to describe. Try this for yourself and see how it works. RDSdraw deletes a field within the outlines of the object previously copied to the Clipboard.

➡ Copying parts of objects. Click on the Copy button with your right mouse button. Then, with your left mouse button, select the part of the object you want to copy to the Clipboard.

➡ Cutting an object to the Clipboard. Click on the Copy button with your right mouse button, and then select the object you want to cut with the right mouse button. The object will be cut to the Clipboard. From there you can paste it to another part of the drawing space.

DELETING

To delete all the contents on the drawing space, click on the CLR button.

LOADING

You can load any TGA graphics file in the current subdirectory. Follow these steps:

❶ Click on the Load button.

❷ Delete the word NONAME by pressing Backspace.

❸ Enter the name of the file you want to load and press ↵ twice. For example, enter **volcano** ↵ ↵ to open the VOLCANO.TGA file.

GENERATING

If you are satisfied with your draft, click on the OK button, then follow these steps:

❶ If you want to save the first picture, answer the first question by pressing Y, change the given file name (without adding an extension), and press ↵.

❷ If you want to produce a stereogram straightaway, answer the first question by pressing N, choose the type of stereogram you want to produce by pressing →, then press ↵ twice.

RDSdraw will display the stereogram and ask "Do you want to save it now?"

❸ If you want to save the completed stereogram as a TGA file, press ↵, change the suggested file name if necessary (again, don't add an extension), and press ↵ twice.

tip After you exit RDSdraw, you can find the TGA file you saved in step 3 in the \MAGIC subdirectory. You can then view and print this file by using a graphics program such as PaintShop Pro or CorelDRAW.

BACKGROUND COLORS

In a picture, elements drawn with colors in the fields -7 to -1 appear to have receded to the background of the stereogram, with elements in the -7 color furthest in the background. You can change background colors by clicking on a new field.

FOREGROUND COLORS

The color black (number 0) represents the medium three-dimensional layer. You can draw elements with colors number 1 to 8, which appear further toward the foreground—the higher the number, the further forward.

3-D FILLING STYLE

Normally, RDSdraw produces exponential gradient fills with its 3-D tools. The idea here is to heighten the three-dimensional effect. However, you can alter this by clicking on the word

ROUND, which changes the setting to LINEAR. RDSdraw will now produce linear gradient fills with color layers of the same width.

tip Gradient fills usually begin with the currently selected drawing color and end with color number 0. To chose another color, just click with the right mouse button on the field of the color you want.

GETTING THE LATEST VERSION OF RDSDRAW

Finally, I thought you'd like to know a little about RDSdraw and how to get the latest version of it.

RDSdraw was developed by Johannes Schmid and released as public-domain software. "Public-domain software" means you can give the program to others—your friends, for example—but if you like RDSdraw, send the author some money. In return, he'll send you the latest version of the program. RDSdraw will definitely be developed further.

Here's the author's address:

Johannes Schmid

Rudliebstraße 50

D-81925 Munich, Germany

Don't forget to include your address.

Sybex Stereogram Gallery

55

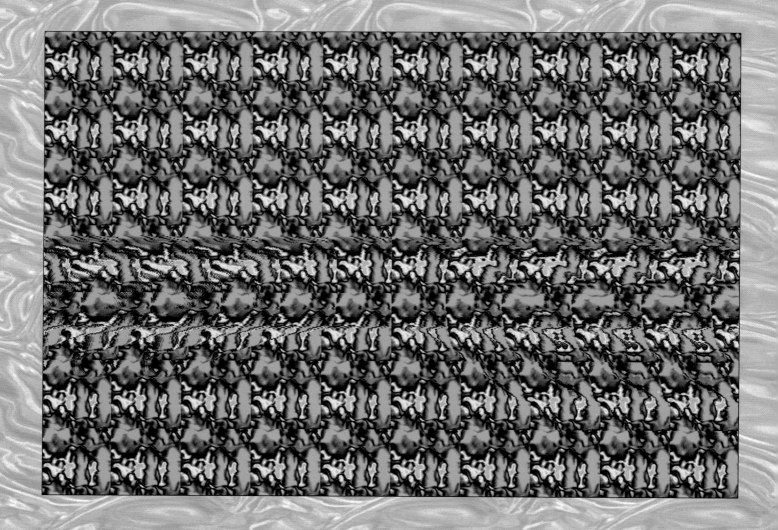

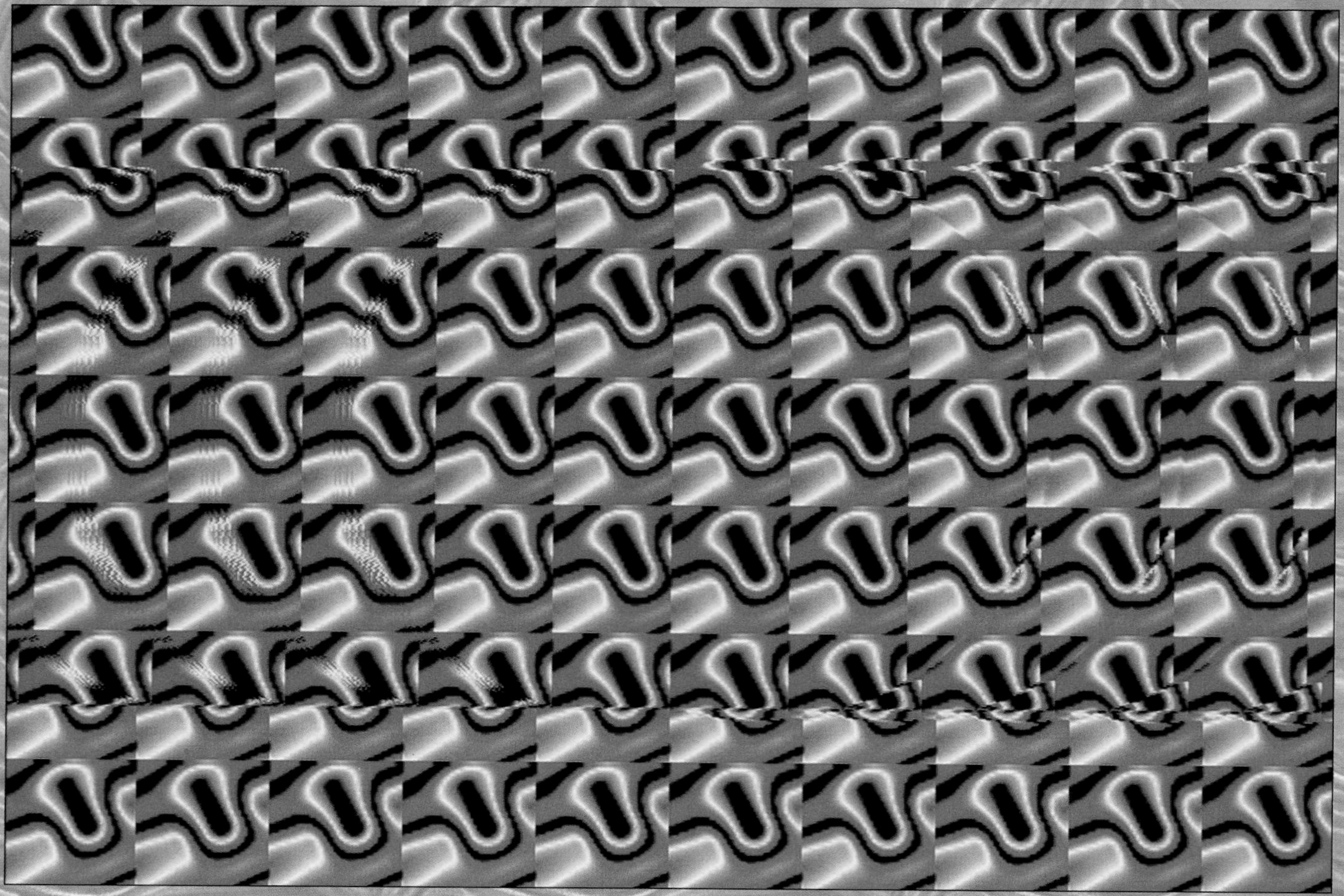

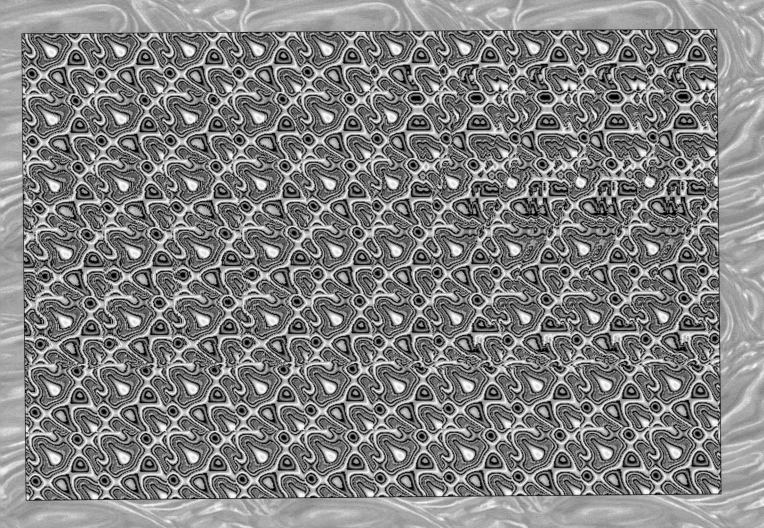

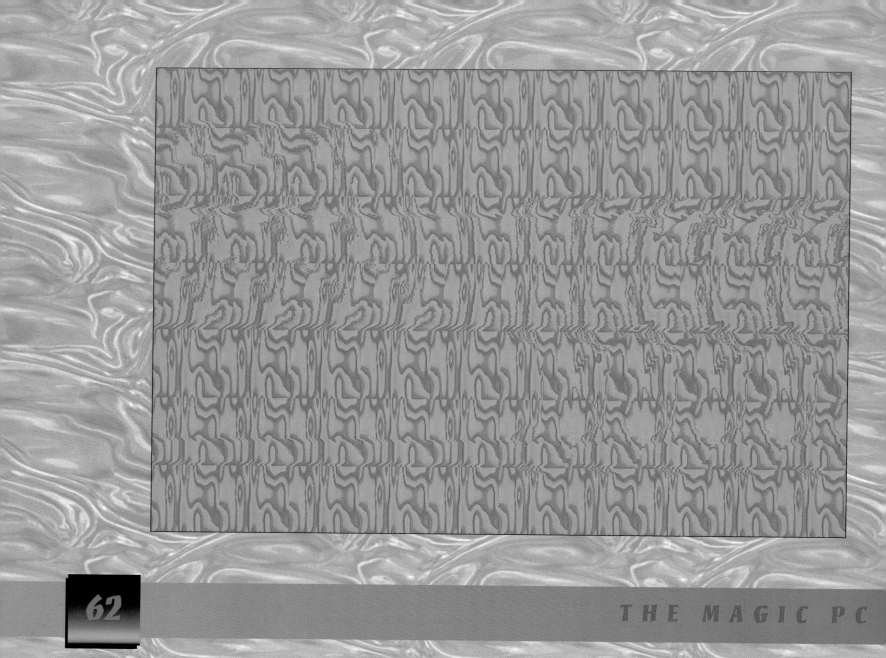

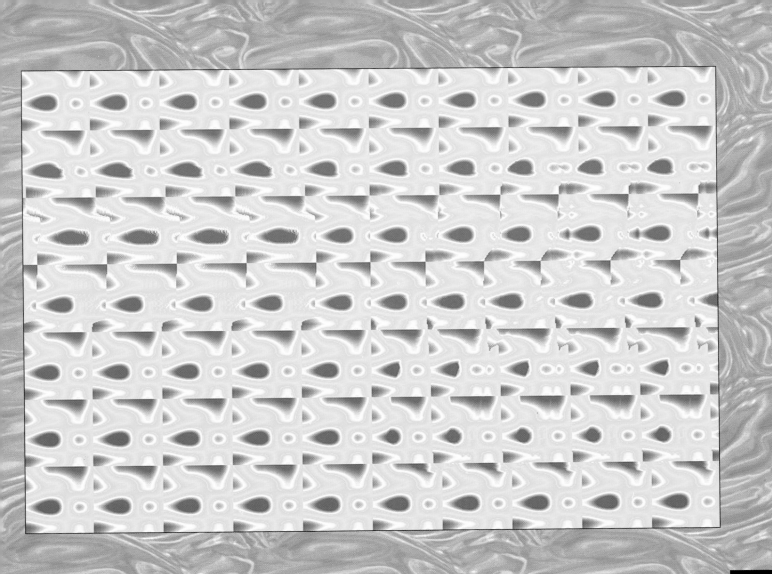

ABOUT THE COMPANION DISK

Warranty

SYBEX warrants the enclosed disk to be free of physical defects for a period of ninety (90) days after purchase. If you discover a defect in the disk during this warranty period, you can obtain a replacement disk at no charge by sending the defective disk, postage prepaid, with proof of purchase to:

SYBEX Inc.
Customer Service Department
2021 Challenger Drive
Alameda, CA 94501
(800)227-2346
Fax: (510) 523-2373

After the 90-day period, you can obtain a replacement disk by sending us the defective disk, proof of purchase, and a check or money order for $10, payable to SYBEX.

Disclaimer

SYBEX makes no warranty or representation, either express or implied, with respect to this software, its quality, performance, merchantability, or fitness for a particular purpose. In no event will SYBEX, its distributors, or dealers be liable for direct, indirect, special, incidental, or consequential damages arising out of the use of or inability to use the software even if advised of the possibility of such damage.

The exclusion of implied warranties is not permitted by some states. Therefore, the above exclusion may not apply to you. This warranty provides you with specific legal rights; there may be other rights that you may have that vary from state to state.

Copy Protection

None of the programs on the disk is copy-protected. However, in all cases, reselling or making copies of these programs without authorization is expressly forbidden.